GETTING GORGEOUS

Deborah McKinlay was born in New Zealand but has lived in Britain since 1985. She is a columnist for *Esquire*, a contributing editor to *Cosmopolitan* and writes for *Vogue* and the *Guardian*. She is the author of *Love Lies, Sex Secrets, Bosom Buddies* and *Man Handling*.

She lives in the West Country.

GETTING GORGEOUS

Deborah McKinlay

HEADLINE

First published in 1998
by HEADLINE BOOK PUBLISHING

First published in paperback in 1999
by HEADLINE BOOK PUBLISHING

10 9 8 7 6 5 4 3 2 1

ISBN 0 7472 5859 7

Designed by Isobel Gillan

Typeset by
Letterpart Limited, Reigate, Surrey

Printed and bound in Great Britain by
Mackays of Chatham PLC, Chatham, Kent

HEADLINE BOOK PUBLISHING
A division of Hodder Headline PLC
338 Euston Road
London NW1 3BH

This book is for **Chicken**
and Sweetie

30 things **women** **do in pursuit of** **beauty,** shoes **and** happiness

in no particular order

You can buy a certain amount of happiness, Pearl
But, you know somethin, Pearl, it never tastes as good as the stuff you make yourself
PEARLS OF WISDOM

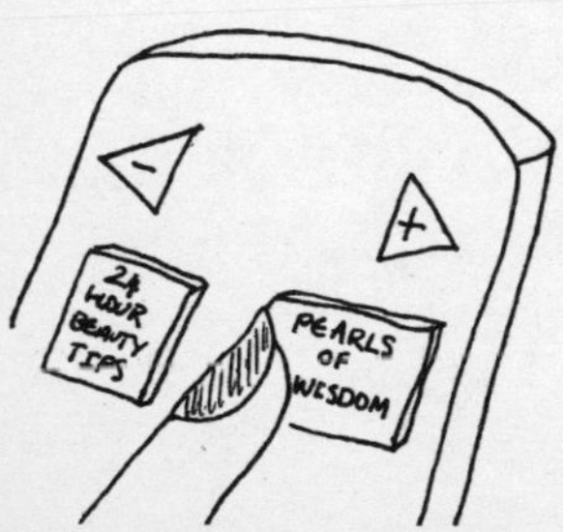
24 HOUR BEAUTY TIPS
PEARLS OF WISDOM

Now Available Great hair days. Limited supply.

one

dolling up

Sometimes a woman buys herself an outfit that would look much better on someone who is a lot taller than she is. Ideally this person would be tanned. Anyway, one day, when the woman is going somewhere and she hasn't got anything new to wear (Going Somewhere, other than a meeting with an accountant, is always enhanced by something new to wear), she drags this outfit out and has a bit of a try on. Sometimes she decides to ignore its defects and wear it. Women always regret a decision like this the instant it is too late to go back and change.

Things Women Have Worn And Regretted The Instant It Was Too Late To Go Back And Change

- *A stretchy mini-skirt which creeps up, thus necessitating constant tugging at the sides*
- *A bustier (ditto the constant tugging at the sides)*
- *Knickers that wedge (ditto)*
- *Stockings that slip (ditto)*

- *False eyelashes, false nails, a wig (ditto, ditto, ditto)*
- *Spike-heeled shoes*
- *A very wide-brimmed and easily wind-swept hat*
- *Firm-fitting trousers which look fine when the wearer is standing but which cling in an unseeming manner to the thigh when the wearer is sitting down*
- *Something see-through*
- *Something very, very, dressy and suitable for, say, the Rose Ball in Monte Carlo, to somewhere other than the Rose Ball in Monte Carlo*

After an incident like this a woman is not usually tempted to go out in anything other than a black trouser suit (bought four years ago in a sale) for quite some time. A woman's Going Somewhere occasion tends to be spoilt if she feels that she is not looking her best.

Of course a woman *can* have a perfectly nice time when she is not Looking Her Best but this nice time is most likely to involve a darkened cinema and another woman.

Nothing to wear is only part of Not Looking Her Best. These are some of the other elements:

- *Hair (not going right)*
- *Skin (sallow/dry/lined/pale/blotchy/spotty)*
- *Weight (gained)*
- *Water (retained)*

It should be noted that most of the above are only visible to the naked eye of the woman concerned and people who work in the beauty business. They are never visible to boyfriends or husbands. This is particularly true if these boyfriends or husbands have been ready to leave the house for longer than fifteen minutes.

The truth is that a woman usually has a much nicer time when none of these problems is besetting her. In fact, very few women want to go to a fabulously fancy restaurant, no matter how marvellous the mousse, no matter how divine the decor, no matter how much effort their boyfriends or husbands have gone to to get the reservation, if their hair is all flat on top, their thighs are up a size, their eyes are liney, and they haven't got any shoes that go with this frock. Boyfriends and Husbands should note that saying things like . . .

- *you-look-absolutely-fine-now-come-on*
- *nobody's-going-to-notice-we're-already-late*
- *it-doesn't-matter-what-you-look-like-we've-got-to-go*

definitely will not help the situation at all

Apart from the fabulously-fancy-restaurant scenario, there are some other things that women don't want to do in circumstances like these. For example:

- *Bump into a potential new boyfriend*
- *Bump into an ex-boyfriend*
- *Bump into a boyfriend's ex-girlfriend*
- *Go to a school reunion*

There are not many women who've never ducked into a shop doorway in order to avoid a situation like this or worse:

- *Bumping into a woman who always looks her best and is a real cow*

BROAD ASIDES
A Slice-of-Sofa Life Production
All Female Cast
No-o I wouldn't say you looked fat

For Hire
Re-conditioned
bodies. Immaculate
condition. Excellent
weekend rates.

two

getting girly

In spring a woman's shins get her attention. These bits of a woman's limbs often degenerate into a condition that looks distinctly reptilian during the months when it's dark around 4p.m. and woolly-weave opaques are regularly worn.

But on the day that she is woken by the sound of the dawn chorus and the sight of dappled sunlight on the duvet, a woman begins to think about going 'sheer' or 'bare' in the near future. Shaving days are here again. After a woman has broken out her razor and taken to her calves she slathers a bit of body lotion on her newly nude knees. She is pleased with the sensation of smoothness beneath. She's begun the Getting Girly process. This process is not just a spring thing. Other common instigators are:

- *Special occasions*
- *Holidays*
- *Men*

Getting Girly usually involves tying up the bathroom for quite some time. Apart from shaving her shins, these are some of the things that a woman is doing in there:

- *Shampooing*
- *Conditioning*
- *Soaking*
- *Exfoliating*
- *Depilating*
- *Treating*
- *Tweezing*
- *Trimming*
- *Cleansing*
- *Toning*
- *Moisturising*

When the woman emerges from the bathroom, all steamy clean and silky, she shuts herself in the bedroom for quite some time. This is what she's doing in there:

- *Drying*
- *Filing*
- *Spraying*
- *Perfuming*
- *Painting*
- *Tipping her head upside down and shaking it*

Then she selects her underwear. Selecting underwear is key Getting-Girly-wise. A woman does not tend to feel too girly in time-of-the-month knickers. After this level of preparation she goes for the top-drawer variety.

Examples Of Top-Drawer-Variety Underwear

- *A lacy bra with little pads at the sides for enhancing cleavage*
  (These little pads sometimes slip and give the game away so the woman might need to stick 'em in with a bit of double-sided)
- *Something skimpy of fake leopardskin*
- *A corset or a basque*
  (Corsets and basques used to be made with whale bones but in these enlightened times whales aren't called upon to die for such fripperies so they are made with pieces of plastic instead. As a rule these pieces of plastic have quite sharp ends which escape their lacy encasings and stick into the wearer just beneath the rib bone)
- *A black satin body*
  (A body is something equipped with 'poppers'. In addition to embarrassing popping possibilities, these little devils involve the wearer in Olympic-level gymnastics should she unwisely undo them in order to pee)

- *Something red*
  (Often a bit scratchy)
- *A garter belt*
- *Knickers ranging from thongs to lacy-legged french jobs*
  (Some of these will be silk but most will be made of something that a pamphlet about yeast infections would advise against)

After underwear, all the woman has to do is finish dressing, apply her make-up and adorn herself with jewellery ... and men sometimes wonder why we can't keep this up the whole time.

Old Image Going cheap.

three

consulting a professional

Most women who are not very wealthy, which is most women, are experts in the DIY or DI for a Friend school of beauty. This means that they have at some point in their lives:

- *Cut or had a fringe cut with a pair of kitchen scissors*
- *Plucked eyebrows*
- *Made a face mask out of fruit, yoghurt, oatmeal or a combination of these ingredients*
- *Made hair conditioner out of all the above plus beer and eggs*
- *Put false eyelashes on someone*
- *Attempted a french plait*
- *Made a skirt*
- *Made something that looks like a skirt, or maybe a bikini top, out of something that looks like a scarf*
- *Dyed shoes/hair/t-shirts*
- *Tried to make their eyes look more almond-shaped with shading*
- *Experimented with different clothing combos in an attempt to create a latest-look look, such as they have just seen in a magazine, on the telly, or on some woman at the train station.*

There are times when a woman gets fed up with all this faffing about. She decides to Consult A Professional. When a woman Consults A Professional she is usually after a Whole New Look which will simplify her life and fit in with her busy schedule. It will definitely not involve putting a tea towel round your neck or holding anything up with safety pins.

A woman can find a Professional New Look Consultant by perusing the back pages of any woman's beauty bible. These are always teeming with advertisements for services which teach a woman how to streamline her beauty regime by only ever wearing the colours of her season and lipstick to match. The problem with these kinds of services is that they are often supplied by a woman who looks suspiciously like she dyes her hair in the privacy of her own kitchen and runs up her skirts on a Singer at the dining-room table. This puts the woman who is after something a bit more slick and city-fied right off.

Luckily, a Professional New Look can be had without ever getting a whiff of anyone's kitchen. The modern woman can always get herself a Makeover. Makeovers are offered by Professional Consultants in department stores. If a woman goes in for one of these she gets to sit on a brightly lit podium while someone makes her eyes look more almond-shaped with shading and passing shoppers have a good shufti on their way to the knickers department. This isn't entirely what a woman wants either. Ideally, she'd like a whole team of Professionals to sort her out head to foot. Well, as it happens, those canny mag and telly folks have picked up on this need.

Nowadays any number of women get to show up at a studio where someone chucks out the entire contents of their make-up bag before pointing out and highlighting their best features. Someone else whips off half their hair and demonstrates the marvels of mousse. And yet another obliging and knowledgeable soul swathes them in berry-coloured velvet, which a) they would never have thought of wearing, and b) you would not know came from M&S (on account of the clever accessorising).

The resultant miracle is broadcast to the nation complete with Before and After images. Lots of women everywhere are agog at the transformation. They have a little hunt through their own wardrobes for anything that's velvet and more or less berry-coloured and then they head for the kitchen and have a little hack at their fringes.

flash us@fab snaps.co.red eye rise

Missing Fame and fortune. Please call any time.

four

being special

A lot of women, but particularly those who are youngish, think that they are Special. They think that their friends are Special too. They think that other people are probably just ordinary Joes, poor things, which must be a bit hellish.

It's not that men never think they are Special. Most men are certain in the knowledge that they are Special. This knowledge is based on a combination of mother-love, having thrashed some other guy at something and the fact that an older woman made a pass at them when they were fifteen. Sometimes a man's certainty of Specialness just has to do with the number of times he was sick after seventeen pints and an Indian takeaway in 1983. Female Specialness is less specific. Often it has more to do with being able to identify with fictional characters than anything actual.

Fictional Characters That Women Have Identified With

- *The heroine in Rebecca*
- *The heroine in The Piano*

- *The heroine in Gone With The Wind*
- *Cinderella*
- *Somebody in Hello magazine*

The point is that not many women identify with Ma Kettle.

Anyway, the youngish woman who is convinced that she is Special often spends quite a lot of time during her twenties and thirties waiting for Special things to happen in her life. A lot of these things have to do with men, money and fabulous careers in the glamour industries.

Sometimes, quite often actually, these things *don't* happen, despite the fact that the woman has splashed out a fait bit of cash on clothes which will be very suitable for when they do. (A woman wants to be looking her best on the day her dreams come true.) In these circumstances a woman comes to the conclusion that she needs a plan. She buys a lottery ticket.

A woman doesn't really think that she'll win the lottery. It's just that she thinks she sort of deserves to, on account of her Specialness, and, anyway, it gives her something to invest some hope in.

Other Things That Women Have Invested Some Hope In:

- *No-diet formulas for weight loss*
- *No-surgery formulas for face lifts*
- *Competitions where you win a wardrobe if you can say why you want to win a wardrobe in thirty witty words or less*
- *Competitions where you win a modelling contract*
- *The second post on Valentine's Day*

When these investments fail a woman is sometimes tempted to create her own Specialness.

Some Things Women Do To Create Their Own Specialness

- *Decide that they are a little bit dyslexic*
- *Decide that they are lactose intolerant*
- *Decide that they are suffering from yeast allergy*
- *Decide that their relationship with their mother is unique*

By and large men don't go to so much trouble if their Specialness needs a boost. They just decide they've got a brain tumour whenever they catch a head cold.

Cash Buyers for visions of the future. Anything considered.

five

looking to the future

Sometimes a woman needs some professional advice with regard to her future. She goes to see a psychic.

Some women aren't interested in things you can't see and touch but an awful lot are. An awful lot more than men.

Things Women Are Interested In That You Can't See Or Touch

- *The power of crystals*
- *The truth of the Tarot*
- *The influence of the stars on our daily lives*
- *The effect of furniture placement on our love lives*
- *Auras*

When a woman goes to see a psychic what she wants is positive, concrete info in the men/money/fabulous-career areas. She tries her best to be very poker-faced and tight-lipped with the psychic so as not to give her too many clues to work with. She gets a bit frustrated if the psychic concentrates on health, long journeys and numbers of children. Still, sometimes, in the middle of a slightly frustrating reading, the psychic says to the woman,

'Do you realize that you are a little bit psychic?'

which gives the woman something to tell the other girls, at least.

Things that you can't see or touch don't appeal only to single women, but a person is less likely to spend £2.39 on Star-Line, rearrange the furniture, or leave little pink stones on lamp tables if there is someone in the immediate vicinity who is going to question her sanity. Also, women often think that a Tarot pack or a newspaper horoscope will help them to glean more information about a man than they can figure themselves from the fact that he hasn't called for over a week.

Part of the reason that a woman believes in the power of a pot plant in her southwest corner to transform her love life is that, as a female, she is just loaded with intuition and instincts. She has lots more of these than most men. A man gets a hint of this if he gets himself caught in the middle of a woman-to-woman between-the-lines communication, or, worse, on the end of an instinct-based interrogation. Anyway, this skill for honing in on the non-physical means that women give a lot more credence to things that aren't-real-as-we-know-it than the average man does. Of course, a woman is not necessarily *absolutely* sure that this particular thing that she is ringing up about is real, still she figures it's worth a shot.

Things That A Woman You Know Thought Were Worth A Shot

- *Having a gold ring, on a string, held over her wrist in order to determine whether her children would be boys or girls*
- *Looking up a man's star sign to see whether he was likely to turn out as rotten as that last Cancerian rat-bag*
- *Adding up a man's birth numbers – ditto*
- *Paying a stranger in a woolly hat working at an open-air market to look at her palm*

Let's say this woman is single. Let's say she meets a man at a party. Let's say this single man is attractive. Let's say that the single woman and the attractive single man strike up a conversation. Let's say that the man says something like,

> ***'You have a lovely aura.'***

Five'll get ya ten the single woman would write him off immediately as a right-looking airy-fairy eejit.

SUPPORT GROUPS FOR OUR TIMES

- Have you ever said:

  'I don't know . . . I think there might be something in it'
  'Sometimes they're quite accurate actually'
  'I'm a real sceptic but I was amazed'
  'There were some things she couldn't have possibly known'

- Do you carry tatty old horoscopes around in your wallet and re-read them on the train?
- Have you spent fruitless half-hours looking for your love line or trying to figure out where your south-west corner is?

Sounds like you'd enjoy a *Hocus Pocus Focus Group*. Keep up with the latest in non-scientific research. Hang out with a friendly bunch of ordinary folks who aren't into incense and caftans but would like to know whether the fact that he writes his 'M's with a triple loop has any bearing on the future of the relationship. Share the story of the night you woke right up because you just *knew* something was wrong (and gasp at the uncanny similarities to other members' experiences).

JOIN NOW. *For further details simply close your eyes and concentrate on whatever it is you want to know.*

Detached man.
Auction Saturday.

six

making an effort to meet a man

Most modern women spend a bit of time outside the couple cocoon. This is not to say that men never spend any time without a partner, it's just that it seems that way, particularly to an ex-wife, ex-fiancée or recently ditched girlfriend. Most women

don't mind life outside the couple cocoon too much. In fact they consider that there are some distinct advantages to the single state. Such as:

- *You only have to deal with your own family*
- *You do not feel guilty if you wear jogging pants for the entire weekend*
- *You can try on all your clothes until there is a huge pile of them on the floor and then say 'I've got nothing to wear' without fear of contradiction*
- *You can eat soup for supper*
- *You never have to watch videos in which men run out from flames brandishing weapons while women with small bottoms scream*
- *You can make face masks out of fruit and put them on while watching videos in which there are stories with feelings, or nice frocks*
- *No one knows if you scratch your car*

Nevertheless, when a woman has decided to walk home, one balmy summer evening, through the park, she is likely to decide that she'd

like a man to hold hands with. This is why. Whenever a woman decides to walk home, one balmy summer evening, through the park, she discovers that The Whole World Is A Couple.

Other Discoveries That Women Make During The Course Of Their Adult Lives

- *Your hair always looks nicest on the day you're due to have it cut*
- *You do not need 42 per cent of the stuff you pack*
- *If you put your pyjamas on straight after your bath someone will come to the door*

On the evening that a woman discovers that The Whole World Is A Couple, wandering arm-in-arm to some fancy restaurant, she sometimes decides to make more effort to meet a man. This kind of thinking can lead to a woman doing something rash. Like:

- *Going on a blind date*
- *Getting all dolled up and going to a party where the wine is warm and the men wear their jacket sleeves pushed up past their elbows*
- *Calling a solicitor with a slim sense of humour and a dodgy line in ties, to whom she was introduced by her sister about fourteen months ago*
- *Having a drink with her ex*
- *Developing total amnesia re her ex's new partner during the course of this drink*
- *Agreeing to a casual supper at a friend's house which a friend of the friend's husband ('He's really nice') will be attending*
- *Travelling halfway across town to a Sainsbury's which has a good reputation cute-bachelor-wise*
- *Posting a cheque for £120 and a membership form to a Dinner Dating Club which advertises for attractive professionals*

When a woman gets home after an excruciatingly embarrassing evening with a geek, or a hideous schlep back from a Sainsbury's packed with squalling kids, or a dinner date with a man in a toupee, or a brain-numbingly boring evening trying to make conversation with someone who has a mania for hang-gliding, or has a vivid mental picture of the way her ex used to explain things to her as if she were a three-year-old ... she decides that she is never going to do anything this rash ever again. She sticks to this resolution until:

- *Three of her closest friends are having babies*
- *She has to spend the entire Christmas break with her parents for the thirty-fifth time*
- *Her youngest sibling gets engaged*

In circumstances like these even the most contented independent might find herself thinking that a Fun In The Sun Singles Holiday doesn't look too bad in the brochure.

For Sale. Gab.
Unwanted gift.

seven

talking

When a man is settled in, with a television and a sofa and something in a can, feeling a bit miffed with the world outside his sitting room, one of the things he doesn't usually want to do is talk. Ideally, he would like it if no one else did this either. If this man has a woman in his life, his ideal is not always attained. When a woman talks about having 'someone to share things with', a lot of what she means is 'someone to talk to'.

Nowadays a talent for communication is recognized as a skill. Lots of women can lick lots of men hands down when it comes to kicking verbal butt. This is one of the reasons that they tend to elevate this particular skill above many others. Another one is that they enjoy it. When women telephone their women friends no introductory gambit is required. One woman just says hello and forty-five minutes later both women are suffering from phone-ear and little sharp pains in the sides of their necks. In circumstances like these the women have to make a plan to get together soon to catch up. At this catch-up they will have plenty to say to each other. This is true even if the catch-up occurs before their necks have stopped hurting.

The thing is, a woman doesn't just talk, she analyses as she verbalises. Also, she expresses herself, asserts herself, explains herself and states her needs. Some women, who are really hooked, validate and empower themselves as well.

Women think that having a talk with a man will be a problem-solving manoeuvre. Also, it will be nice. That is why, one night, when a couple are having a perfectly pleasant time and a woman has had a couple of glasses of red wine, she starts having-a-talk.

Most modern women are not damn fools. They avoid announcing the having-a-talk talk, they just try to slip it in when the man is:

a) not paying too much attention
b) unable to escape

When women talk to each other there are no spaces. When women talk to men there are. Sometimes a woman has to go and say something she doesn't even mean to a man, just to fill up a space. This means that the having-a-talk talk is very rarely problem solving at all. In fact it is problem creating.

You see, a man is not very often of the opinion that he is to blame for very much, and, anyway, even if he is, he's certainly not keen to have this pointed out to him. So if a woman starts talking about a few of her problems, and casually points out that these problems are the result of problems with the man, the man doesn't react well. He gets morose. He gets silent. A morose and silent male and a revved up, determined-to-talk-about-this female are rarely a top combo romantic occasion-wise. The evening is not a success.

After a couple have had an evening like this, the man definitely does not want to talk about it. Actually, he doesn't even want to think about it. Ideally, he'd just like to forget the whole thing.

The next morning, when the woman in this man's life comes quietly downstairs and looks at him with sweet, sad eyes, the man thinks that this ideal is going to be attained.

The man gives the woman a hug.
The woman gives the man a hug.
The woman says, 'Sorry.'
The man says, 'Let's just forget it.'
The woman takes a deep breath . . .

dreams come true@gobstoppers.co.call back city

Misc. Sales
Positive mental attitudes. Bankrupt stock.

eight

reading some popular psychology

Nobody could accuse American Psychologists of being slow to spot a niche in the market.

Some Niches That American Psychologists Have Spotted

- *The need to extend your comfort zone*
- *The need to tend to your inner infant*
- *The need for empowerment*
- *The need to wake up your giant, smell the coffee, connect with love, dance with fear and set it free*

You could accuse American Psychologists of laughing all the way to the bank.

Of course women outside of America, who are not pop or movie stars, are a wee bit sceptical about all this. They consider that it's California Kooky. As a rule, women think it's about half as kooky as a man does. That's why, when a woman is lent an American

Psychologist's book by a friend, she doesn't necessarily leave this book on the bedside table if there is a bloke knocking about. This bloke, though, might realise that the woman had succumbed and read some of the American Psychologist's book (just to see what her friend was on about) if she started saying things like this:

- *My family is dysfunctional*
- *My child has attention-deficit disorder*
- *My issues with my childhood are unresolved*
- *His behaviour is typical of a co-dependent*

Luckily for most men, most women don't succumb quite this far. The average woman just distils the American Psychologist's essential points. Which are:

- *Be kind to yourself*
- *Think positive*
- *Write down everything that's bothering you on a piece of paper and then burn it*
- *Write down everything that's good about you on a piece of paper and then stick it to the bathroom mirror*

For this a woman doesn't need to buy too many books. Women have got each other to keep them on track (very few women have to rely on a sticky label on the bathroom mirror to tell them that they're not fat), which means that those American Psychologists who stick with the power-of-maximising-your-mental-energy formula are usually making a few less trips to the bank than the ones who come up with a theory that relates to romantic relationships. It's men that women really want help with.

When an American Psychologist comes up with something that explains to lovelorn females that the reason they keep putting their hearts and souls into the pursuit of romantic relationships with men who are deeply unattractive, extremely unavailable or homosexual is that they are replaying-the-scripts-of-their-childhood, women lap it up. So do their friends.

Men are usually pretty sceptical, but that's OK, because everybody knows the reason for this is that they are:

- *Commitment-phobic*

Men Free to good
homes.

nine

ditching a man

Occasionally, women apply the spending-spree-clothes-shopping criteria to men. This means that they get all excited about someone until they get him home and discover that he doesn't fit in too well with anything else in their lives. As a general rule once a woman has got a man home she is reluctant to get rid of him. (Men should not get too puffed up about this because the same is true of two-sizes-too-small lime trousers bought in a sale-price frenzy.) A woman usually tries very hard to make the man fit (ditto the trousers). And then she tries to make herself fit him. A lot of women will keep this up even once the whole business is causing them physical pain. (Ditto the trousers.)

Luckily, the smart modern woman gets wise eventually. She decides that she would be happier without the man. (She hangs on to the trousers for a little bit longer.)

When a woman decides that she would be much happier without a man she goes all cold on him. Quite often this has the effect of encouraging the man to make a bit more effort to fit in with the woman's life so everything gets confused for a while, but it also makes the woman feel like she is back in control and so, after a bit, she tells this chap that it's curtains. After a woman has told a chap that it's curtains she usually:

a) worries that she's done the wrong thing
b) decides that he gave her no option
c) becomes convinced that she will never meet anyone else ever again
d) is devastated when she hears that the man has a new girlfriend
e) reverts to a) and c)

All of the above occur within a fourteen-day period.

A woman doesn't always ditch a bloke because she made a mistake bringing him home in the first place. Sometimes two people meet by accident at the launderette. Their relationship progresses fairly smoothly. Soon they are sharing a sofa on a regular basis. One night this man and this woman are on the sofa watching television. The man is feeling content. The woman is feeling . . . nothing.

The man does not know how close he is to having his contented evening completely blown.

This is what has happened: the Love Pie Effect.

When a woman meets a man she gives him her Love Pie. She has baked four and twenty high hopes into this pie. At first a man is a reasonably good guardian of a woman's Love Pie, but, as time goes by, he dashes a few of her high hopes. Every time this happens the woman grabs back a slice of her pie. After a while she is clutching the lot. A man is not aware of this development.

A man, on the other hand, tends only to hand out his pie, tiny slice by tiny slice. Still, if you're nice to him, he lets you keep it. That's why he's quite happy, with his feet up, thinking nothing's amiss till the woman in his life hisses, '*Why are we watching this?*'

Quite soon after the fight that the hissed comment starts, there is a parting of the ways.

The woman, who has engineered this parting, decides that life is going to be much happier and more exciting from now on. As often as not she sets this process off by getting her hair cut and splashing out on something like a pair of two-sizes-too-small lime trousers in a shopping-spree frenzy.

cry for us@outta my hair.co.solo junction

Responsible Lady
companion wanted for
discerning feline.
Non-smoker preferred

ten

kissing cats

You're not meant to kiss cats (ringworm). Women who own cats kiss them all the time. Here are some other things they tend to do:

- *Talk to them*
- *Cook chicken breasts for them*
- *Let them sleep on the bed*

There are women in the world who love labradors or geldings called Sundance but it's a bit hard to keep one of these in a first-floor flat. That's why an urban Miss is most likely to be kissing a cat when she gets back from work in the evenings.

If a man should give a cat a smooch or two, most women would think he was sweet. Nobody has ever heard the expression 'mad cat man'. A woman, though, who loves her moggy, always finds that the crazy lady tag surfaces at some point. This is particularly true if the woman is childless and single.

The childless, single woman-with-a-cat is supposed to be keener to catch a man than her feline-less counterpart is. This theory is based on the claim that she craves cosy domesticity and something to nurture. The fact that she already has somebody to cook chicken breasts for is glossed over by those who adhere to this idea.

Someone proposed the notion that women who love cats do so because the cats always remain baby-sized. And yet plenty of ladies who can't be doing with kids are gaga over something called Ginger. Still, the child-substitute accusation persists. It's nonsense. All moggies' mummies know that the cat *is* their child.

The 'mad' association probably has to do with witches, and cats' connection to all things superstitious. A lot of people think cats are spooky. They're suspicious of them. They find their self-reliance and sudden flights of fancy unnerving.

Sometimes a single, childless, cat-loving woman is going out with a man with this sort of disposition. This man has a lot of other redeeming features. Luckily, there are some things that she can do to help him come to his senses. For example:

- *Not letting the man know that she is basing her opinion of him on her cat's reaction*

- *Not having very long, complicated conversations with the cat in front of him*
- *Not referring to herself as Mummy during even the shortest, most uncomplicated conversation with the cat in front of him*
- *Discouraging the cat from leaping into the man's lap, eyeing him darkly, making slow circling movements and clawing repeatedly at his crotch*

A man who is really keen on a moggy's mummy usually comes round eventually if the above are observed. He may even begin to see that letting a cat sleep between you is sweet. (In a little-bit-mad sort of way.) And anyway, if he doesn't, if he really can't cope with the whole cooking-chicken-breasts-and-investing-a-pet-with-supernatural-powers-of-perception thing, the woman he leaves behind may be sad, she may miss him, but remember this . . . she still has something to kiss.

SUPPORT GROUPS FOR OUR TIMES

- Do you carry a cute little photo of your cat in your wallet that you are too embarrassed to show people even though they are confidently brandishing their boring two-year-old-in-the-bath snaps?
- Do you clam up when somebody is rambling on about some kid's answering-the-phone high jinks just because you suspect that your adorable sitting-right-on-the-page-I-was-reading story wouldn't get the same degree of attention?
- Have you ever defended the cat in a small child vs cat's tail incident?

The *We Are Parents As Well Society* (PAWS) needs members like you. Join us in our fight to be able to call ourselves Mummy in public. Defend our right to talk baby-talk to our own liddle puddykins without risking ridicule. Network with fellow feliners and feel truly supported when you share your 'We used to dress her up as a baby and push her round in the pram' past.

Fill in a membership form without delay.

DON'T FORGET *to sign our attached petition calling for the immediate ban of the Catist expressions Mad Cat Woman and Child Substitute.*

Zest For Life
overhauls. No call-
out charge.

eleven

wallowing

Sometimes a woman is a bit down. She's suffering from low-level angst. Also, she is bored. There is only ever trashy TV on at times like this and best friends are usually busy. This means that the woman is left to her own devices when it comes to finding something to do. These are some things a woman has been meaning to do for ages:

- *Sort through her desk*
- *Chuck out all her old tights*
- *Read some decent novels*
- *Balance her cheque book*
- *Re-pot the plant on the windowsill*
- *Write to her sister*
- *Give the bathroom a good going-over*
- *Find out about yoga classes*

These are some things a woman actually does when she's bored, and suffering from low-level angst:

- *Eats something that has been in a cupboard for a very long time*
- *Practises pulling her hair into different shapes in the hall mirror*

- *Practises putting blusher on the apple of her cheek*
- *Tries on something, as yet unworn, that she bought in a sale two years ago*
- *Flicks discontentedly through an old magazine and re-reads the horoscope to see if it came true*
- *Telephones the phone number under the horoscope*
- *Telephones the phone number under her ex's horoscope*
- *Telephones her ex*

Telephoning your ex when you're a bit down is not often a successful move with regard to alleviating this condition. In fact, sometimes a woman's life gets so full of ex-boyfriends and late-night, low-level-angsty, unsuccessful phone calls to them that her condition deteriorates terribly. You can tell when a woman is in this sort of state because she stops giving a toss about the size of her thighs or the bags under her eyes and she actually stocks up on high-fat, sugar-laden foods so that she won't have to rummage through the cupboards looking for something marzipan, left over from Christmas, to scoff when the ten o'clock news comes on. She begins to favour clothing of the relaxed-fit variety. She watches a *lot* of television. She cries at corny movies. Her sofa is surrounded by the litter of low-mood life. Ashtrays, wine glasses, coffee cups, tabloids opened at the TV page, and empty packets of Pringles and chocolate macadamia nut cookies. She's Wallowing.

Wallowing is not the same as serious distress, such as might result from loss of love, life or job. Wallowing is a shutting-down process. It has to do with feeling that the rewards of diet, exercise, laughing at men's jokes, never going out without mascara, washing your hair every day, and missing *EastEnders* in order to stand about in wine bars, are actually pretty minimal.

It is not only single women who Wallow. Women who live with men do it too. It's just that when a woman who lives with a man is Wallowing she is usually waiting for someone, male, to say something like, 'What's wrong?', thus instigating a nice chat about what ails her. Quite often the lack of such a response leads to an all-out blazing row, which gets the woman off the sofa at least.

Most women get off the sofa eventually anyway. One day they just think enough is enough, slap a bit of blusher on the apple of their cheeks and go shopping. Best friends are usually pretty much in evidence at the time.

Nearly New Fresh start. Hardly used.

twelve

starting over

Things That A Woman Has Vowed To Do Every Day From Now On

- *Walk to work*
- *Drink eight glasses of water*
- *Sit-ups*

These sorts of vows are associated with New Beginnings. Women are big fans of these. Here are some typical Female New Beginnings:

- *Deciding to save some money*
- *Deciding to grow fresh herbs on the windowsill*
- *Deciding always to wear a hat in the sun*
- *Deciding to read more/get up earlier/drink less caffeine and eat fruit instead of chocolate at four o'clock every afternoon*

The good thing about these kinds of New Beginnings is that they don't very often progress to the middle and end stages so women get to make lots of new ones all the time.

Some New Beginnings are sparked off by a change of season. An example of this would be making a decision to apply body lotion after every bath and have regular pedicures (spring), and another would be the New Wardrobe New Beginning.

The New Wardrobe New Beginning has to do with the desire to 'pare down' and get organized and ensure that you have something reasonable to wear, that you can find and not have to iron, on a Thursday when you've overslept. Ideally this thing would go with some shoes that you already own. Women tend to invest most effort into this endeavour on the day that they get their winter clothes out.

Sometimes one sees a television or magazine item about a woman who has one of those walk-in wardrobes where all the clothes are hung in rows, the sweaters are swathed in tissue, and the shoes have little individual box shelves. Sometimes these shelves slide. The woman in question is usually the wife of a deposed dictator, a thrice-divorced movie star, or someone who used to read the weather on GMTV. She does not represent life as we generally know it.

Other Things These Women Have Which Do Not Represent Life As We Generally Know It

- *Personal trainers*
- *Lawyers with whom they lunch*
- *Very large glamorous photos of themselves, conspicuously displayed*
- *Regular pedicures*

Anyway, for most women a New Wardrobe New Beginning does not involve carefully removing the contents of a couple of padded hangers and donating them to a favourite charity.

When, on a chilly Sunday afternoon, a woman drags a suitcase out from under the bed, dusts off two black wool coats that have been lingering in the hall closet since spring, and tugs a couple of pullovers from the shelf in the spare room, she usually discovers that there is a distinct absence of delicately scented tissue paper in her life.

The woman dumps all this gear on the bed. She remembers reading somewhere that you are meant to sort it into clearly marked piles: Never Wear, Keep Till Next Year and Bonfire.

She spends the next hour and a half trying on things she'd forgotten she had with other things to see if they'll go, searching for hats and scarves that she's sure she had last winter, and making a Put Away Later pile. It is very rare for a charity shop to have a bonanza day as a result of these efforts. But that's all right because in the course of her pottering the woman has decided to:

- *Take the stairs instead of the lift*
- *Grow her fringe out*

and

- *Give up arguing with her mother*

stick with it@resolutions kept.co.determination

Not too slim,
pessimistic woman.
Seeks similar, for
fun bitching sessions.

thirteen

being more assertive

Women want to be liked. They think that they will be liked if they are nice to people. Quite often a woman is nice to people who wouldn't like her if she bought them a Ferrari. A woman smiles at heaving bores that her husband has been rude to. In fact, a woman doesn't even need a husband to find herself smiling at some heaving bore who is bending her ear at a party, she can manage it all on her own. Here are some examples, in addition to heaving-bore scenarios, of things a woman does when she's being nice:

- *Says thank you to a hairdresser who has just turned her head into a giant blackberry*
- *Says please to a waitress with an attitude you could freeze peas on*
- *Buys an outfit she can't afford from a sales assistant with an expression that says 'You-can't-afford-it'*
- *Makes cups of tea for two workmen in her house. These workmen are doing no work whatsoever*
- *Says 'fine' when the masseur who is causing her excruciating pain asks her how she's feeling*
- *Leaves a quid in the dish left by a smarmy lavatory attendant*
- *Gives a Christmas bonus to a binman she hasn't seen since Easter*
- *Overtips a bad-tempered cabbie*

In addition to the above, the successful career woman:

- *Gives a birthday present to her assistant who is consistently useless*
- *Can't bring herself to fire someone who is consistently useless and rude*

Women have done all this being nice before they even get to relationships with men.

Most women at some stage in their adult lives have run themselves ragged over a man who is a rat-bag. This means that they have done things like consistently sighing and saying yes to a man who consistently calls and says, 'Can I come over at 11 p.m.?' Women know that this is a mistake in terms of their dignity but they can't help it. Fortunately, most women learn from their rat-bag mistakes, eventually. They only make them once or twice thereafter. Unfortunately, apart from rat-bags, there are nerds for women to say yes to. This means that most women have had dinner with someone they feel very, very sorry for.

After a while a woman generally comes to the conclusion that this sort of behaviour isn't nice at all. It's wimpish. She decides that life will be better all round if she sends back the very next salad she didn't order. She decides to be more assertive.

The woman who has decided to be more assertive doesn't usually find that ages and ages pass before a husband says, 'Have I got any clean socks?', or an assistant at the tights counter ignores her for ten minutes. This means that she often gets to put her more-assertive-skills into practise before she has practised them very much at all. Sometimes she's not very good at them yet. She gets a little bit shrill. Her voice goes from wimp to witch in a matter of minutes.

A husband or tights-counter assistant tends to react to wimpy-witchy shrillness as though they were placating someone with several loose marbles. The woman senses that her assertiveness has gone a bit astray.

After an incident like this a woman sometimes gives up on being more assertive for a while. When she needs to let off steam she gets together with a friend and says things like, 'Has she seen what she looks like from the back?', about another woman who is probably very nice.

Free upon collection
Fascination with flamenco.

fourteen

signing up for a course in something

Here are some words that appear in the titles of informative tomes that women buy:

- *Herbal*
- *Pen*
- *Pot*
- *Stencil*
- *Stitch*
- *Style*
- *Oil*
- *Colour*
- *Water*
- *Camera*
- *Kitchen*

These are words that relate to hobbies. Hobbies make people happy. This is especially true if the hobby is stuck to and the person becomes proficient at it. Young modern women take up hobbies with a vengeance, then . . . they take up something else. A woman tends to forget this on the day that she announces to her friends, boyfriend, husband or mother that she is taking up cross-stitch, rambling or oil painting. She says, 'I've always wanted to do it.'

When women say this sort of thing to mothers, mothers sometimes scoff a bit and remind them about dropping out of karate when they were ten. Boyfriends and husbands nod interestedly as if they were listening to every word and are not caught out until they sit on a tapestry kit and say, 'What *is* this?' Friends often get quite keen on the whole business and decide that they have always wanted to do whatever it is too.

The thing is that pursuing a hobby at home can get a little dull. Plus, informative tomes are notoriously hard to follow. So the initial enthusiasm often wanes fairly quickly and it isn't long before boyfriends, husbands, flatmates, friends and mothers are tripping over easels in the hallway on a regular basis.

One day a woman finds a leaflet among her letters. This leaflet is jam-packed full of courses. Lots of these courses are in things that a woman has always wanted to do.

When a woman signs up for a course in something she has always wanted to do, which takes place once a week somewhere halfway across town, she always talks a friend into signing up too. She does this for two reasons. One is that she is faintly suspicious that everyone else attending ceramic-painting classes will be deeply unattractive, and the other is to *make* herself go.

Women do not always see a connection between their level of commitment to something and the fact that they feel the need for someone else to *make* them go at the outset. This connection usually becomes obvious around course-week four when one of the women has to work late and the other one discovers that a new series of ER is starting.

Luckily, people who teach ceramic painting, samba dancing and interior decorating have caught on to this pattern. So nowadays a woman doesn't have to spend fourteen interminable Tuesday evenings in a draughty hall before she gets a proficiency certificate. These days a woman can go on an Intensive Session Of Lessons. These take place over several days in delightful surroundings. They are the perfect way to spend several days when you can't find anyone to lie on a beach in Greece with you.

When women sign up for an Intensive Session Of Lessons somewhere delightful they tell the people who are too busy to go to Greece with them all about it. Everyone agrees that it sounds terrific. The brochure insists that it is. Still the woman has one misgiving. It is this. She is absolutely certain that all the other people there will be deeply unattractive.

By the time women get back from four days of Tuscan Culinary they have usually met one other attractive woman (with whom they lose touch within approximately ten weeks), a few ordinary folks and a man with whom there is something very wrong. This man is still calling eighteen months later.

Obituary
Once-beloved black hipster flares. Now sadly passé.

fifteen

following fashion

All women reach an age when they say, 'I can't be bothered with fashion any more. I just wear what suits me.' As a general rule they say this about twenty years before it comes true.

When a woman says 'I've got nothing to wear' what she means is 'I've got nothing *fashionable* to wear'. Anybody who doubts how much a woman dislikes having nothing fashionable to wear need only note the expression on her face when she makes this announcement.

It is true that there are not many women over the age of eighteen who are total slaves to fashion. Very few women have the inclination, let alone the cash, to rush out and splash out on everything that appears on the catwalks. It is only the fashion In Crowd who actually use words like:

- *deconstruction*
- *asymmetric*
- *shjooshjee (pronounced shjooshjee)*

when describing frocks. But no matter how determined a woman is to stick with what suits her, it is a rare one who's not tempted to try something deconstructed with an asymmetric hemline and a bit of shjoosh once she's seen it plastered all over the beauty bibles and the High Street windows.

Lots of women do get smart and stick mainly to

- *classics*
  just alternating their black long-lines with their dark grey crops from
- *season to season*
  but the smartest of these women are not above the odd Following Fashion fiasco.

It's like this. A woman has just had a haircut which is reasonably fantasy fulfilling in that it does not make her look like her mother or a sports star from the seventies, so she is in a pretty good mood. She is wearing something in which she feels fairly slim and this adds to her general joie de vivre. Credit possibilities are burning a hole in her pocket. She hits the town. Before you know it she's bought something. Something new and New Look. Something that makes her feel young. Something that makes her feel hip. Something that makes her feel in with the fashion In Crowd. It is not until she gets this thing home that she really faces up to the fact that it is pink. Very pink.

Sometimes the woman wears this pink thing. Quite often actually, which is why the world is full of women giggling at old snapshots of themselves and saying, 'I can't believe I wore that.'

Some Things That People Can't Believe They Wore

- *Clogs*
- *Bandeau Tops*
- *Skirts which created an instant connection in onlookers between the words thighs and thunder*
- *Shoulder pads*
- *Leggings*

The smart mature woman who has outgrown the above (and now says 'I can't believe they're wearing those again'), and currently owns a nice selection of long-line things in black, tends to leave her pink purchase lingering at the back of her wardrobe most of the time. It is ages before she can bring herself to part with it. Finally she decides that pink is really passé and she shoves the thing into an Oxfam bag. Four minutes later pink comes roaring back into fashion and the beauty bibles are full of people looking wonderful in it. The woman is not tempted for at least two months.

FAIRY GODMOTHERS FOR OUR TIMES
You will already own everything on this season's IN list
VOGUE * IN * VOGUEST
• JOGGING PANTS
• OLD BRIDESMAID SHOES
• JUMPERS THAT HAVE GONE BAGGY
• BIG TATTY HANDBAGS
• M+S KNICKERS
• TOO-TIGHT SKIRTS FROM CHAIN STORES
• VERY LONG BLACK OPAQUE TIGHTS
your wishes answered@wardrobe crisis.co.brokesville

Dropped S/F shopper.
Vicinity of High
Street.

sixteen

shopping

Modern women have heard the expression Shopping Therapy. They don't need an explanation of what it means. Women enjoy shopping. It's fun to wander from department to department fingering fabric and trying on unlikely outfits. And even if this particular expedition doesn't turn up the trousers that make your legs look longer, the throw that transforms your sofa, or a lip gloss that lasts, there is always something else that a woman needs. A woman's shopping needs tend to alternate between House and Clothes.

Examples of things that a woman in House Shopping Phase has needed:

- *A large yellow jug (to go in a recess)*
- *Small pillows with lace on them that go on beds*
- *Chenille throw rugs*
- *Tie backs (for curtains)*
- *A pair of matching, oval, fabric-covered picture frames*
- *A brass faucet in the shape of a swallow*
- *Little dishes (for serving peanuts or olives in)*

- *A triangular shelf with a little triangular cupboard above it (for a corner)*
- *Plant containers that look like old tin baths*
- *A perspex waste-paper basket*
- *Two jars of brightly coloured foreign foodstuffs floating in oil*
- *A slatted wooden bathmat*

Examples of things that a woman in a Clothes Shopping Phase has needed:

- *A piece of flowery material that you wrap around your hips on the beach*
- *A fabric rose that you wear in your hair*
- *A chiffon scarf with butterflies on it*
- *Lacy tights*
- *An orange string bag*
- *Leopardskin leggings*
- *Tortoiseshell beads*
- *A thin belt made of fake snakeskin*
- *A wide belt with a very big buckle*
- *A beret*
- *A frock with an asymmetric neckline*
- *A top with a drawstring neckline*
- *Big silver hoop earrings*
- *Something purple*
- *A jacket made of fake fur*
- *A skirt made of suede*
- *Some sunglasses like the stars are wearing*

These lists don't cover tapestry cushions, wedgie shoes, bread boards shaped like lemons, bathroom mirrors decorated with papier mâché fish, crocheted cardies or things with feather trims. These lists don't even start on clogs or tissue-box covers. These lists hardly scratch the surface.

Sometimes a woman goes shopping in a sale for something she needs. Quite often this is the reason that she owns a bread board shaped like a lemon and a very big, cream, feather-trimmed hat. The thing about sale shopping is that even if bread boards shaped like lemons and very big cream feather-trimmed hats were definitely not on your list of needs this morning, a snip price like £2.99 or £29.99 can sometimes get you thinking. Also, since lots of other women have gone shopping in the sale, you know that you have to make your mind up lickity split.

Holiday shopping is, on the other hand, a bit more leisurely. A holiday shop is when you spend a pleasant afternoon wandering from stall to stall in some market because it's a bit cloudy and the men are windsurfing. On this expedition you always discover that for the

bargain price of . . . well you're not sure exactly but it's a bargain, you can buy a throw that will transform your sofa, a large yellow jug and squillions of flowery things to wrap around your hips at the beach. In circumstances like these a woman generally uncovers a bit of a latent need for some hand-tooled footwear as well.

When a woman has lugged back to her self-contained holiday apartment fourteen things that she is going to have to find room for in her already overstuffed suitcases, she feels terrific. Shopping Therapy.

SUPPORT GROUPS FOR OUR TIMES

- Have you ever owned espadrilles with a crissy-crossy bit up the calves? What about wedgies, patent loafers, jelly shoes, three-inch stilettos, neon trainers or velvet slip-ons with curly toes, funny little dented heels and curly-up tongue bits at the front such as a gay man might have worn in the court of Louis XIV?
- Do you currently own several items from the list above *plus* Moroccan slippers and a pair of something fetching in *faux* leopardskin?
- Can you drone on endlessly about the usefulness of having flat brown shoes in three different styles?

Why not join *The Imelda Club*?

Meet others who believe that happiness comes with a heel. Share experiences such as 'Why I bought the matching handbag'. Ensure a sympathetic ear when you've blown the gas money on some lovely little ballerina slippers in silver.

APPLY TODAY. *(Enclose a recent photograph of a footwear item which did not fit you on the day you bought it.)*

Birth Announcement
Baby soft
complexion. Mother
doing beautifully.

seventeen

buying beauty products

For a woman Looking Lovely is often a major step towards Feeling Terrific. That's why lots of women everywhere are prepared to invest so much time and energy into it. Not to mention any number of £23.99s. An awful lot of people who've made an awful lot of money in the Looking Lovely business are grateful for this fact.

Some Ways That People Have Made An Awful Lot Of Money In The Looking Lovely Business

- *Combining the words Cellulite and Banish*
- *Translating perfectly ordinary words into French*
- *Using completely made-up words that end in 'sphere' or 'zone' such as one might have heard at some point on an early episode of Star Trek*
- *Putting the words Natural and/or Rain Forest on a label*
- *Putting something made of squished-up bananas into a very nice woody kind of bottle which looks good in the bathroom*

- *Putting a picture of someone who looks like Claudia Schiffer looking like she always looks on a bottle of something that looks like water*
- *Developing anything which has a light texture, pleasant perfume, pretty colour, no sticky after-effects, is easily applied and has some visible effect (within twenty-one days) on fine eye-lines or flyaway hair*
- *Developing a new improved version of the above*

Women are not fools, they do not believe every word of an advertising campaign that promises the banishment of free radicals. In fact they are not absolutely sure what a free radical is. Still, if the banishment of free radicals led to baby-soft skin à la the girl who's getting paid £10,000 to grace the advertising campaign, £23.99 would be a bargain, wouldn't it? Cheaper than laser surgery anyhow. Cheaper than shoes. That is why a woman who has just spent her lunch-hour sunbathing and smoking cigarettes invests in something that reduced wrinkles in a lab test in France. (The results of this lab test are amply illustrated by a little grainy, liney picture and a contrasting, magnified, not so grainy, liney picture.) At best it will work, at worst it won't and by the time she's sure of this something new and improved will be claiming to replace your retinol.

Of course lots of women do not spend their lunch-hours sunbathing on account of the detrimental effect it has on your retinol. The Looking Lovely business has not been slow to come up with a few new improved versions of things which make up for this fact. The modern non-sunbathing female can get herself a sunkissed skintone in no time. All she needs is a hot bath, some body lotion, an exfoliating mitt, some cream that costs £8.99 and a prosthetic hand for applying it to her back.

So whenever a woman is feeling a bit drab, a bit dull-eyed, a bit lacking in lustre, she can drop by any department store with a quarter of the cash she'd have to muster for a frock and take her pick of pick-me-up lotions and potions. She is only a teeny bit put off by the fact that the be-smocked Looking Lovely representative, to whom she eventually hands her cash, is wearing two ton of slap and has skin which looks like it's been round the block with an army of free radicals.

New Season's Faces
Ready to put on.
Brochure available.

eighteen

buying make-up

Women know that make-up is magic. Some men who've seen some women mascara-less have an inkling of this too. It's not that lots of women aren't lovely *au naturel* it's just that once they've seen what concealer can do their completely concealer-less days are often fairly few.

Apart from concealer these are some of the other make-up items that women buy regularly:

- *Foundations*
- *Pencils*
- *Blushers*
- *Eyeshadows*
- *Mascaras*
- *Nail polishes*

This list represents the absolute basics. A woman has more than one of each of these items because, for example, some pencils are for lips, some for brows and some for eyes, some mascaras are waterproof, some are lengthening and some are volumising . . . you begin to see the sort of bulk sales your average mascara-maker can look forward to. In addition to the absolute basics, these are some of the other make-up not-so-must-haves that an otherwise sensible woman has shelled out for (and still has lurking around somewhere):

- *Some stuff for giving your face an all-over shine*
- *Some stuff for stopping your face from getting an all-over shine*
- *Mascara for hair*
- *Glitter for cheeks, chests and upper arms*
- *White eyeshadow*
- *Black lipstick*
- *A french manicure kit*

A woman who is under twenty buys this sort of thing because her friend has got some and a woman who is over twenty buys it because she saw it in a magazine (and also her friend has got some). In addition to these influences there is another factor in the masses of make-up-purchasing trends that affects most females. It's this. The Palette.

Every season has its own Palette, which is awfully good news for the people who thought of calling red 'poppy'. In spring and summer when, as everybody knows, women are all clear-skinned, gently tanned and glowy eyed, they need:

- *Some creamy blusher in Rose*
- *Some highlighting powder in Burnished Bronze*
- *Some waterproof mascara in Caviar*
- *A lip pencil in Nudo*
- *A nail polish in Mocha*
- *A lip gloss in Coral Dew*
- *An eye-shades duo in Tawny/Sierra*

and, maybe, a touch of eye-liner in Smudge, foundation in Cacao and Kumquat lipstick for evenings. Whereas in the wintry months they need:

- *Powder blusher in Tawny*
- *Lengthening mascara in Gris*
- *Under make-up primer in Sheer Light*
- *Foundation in Ivory Sand*
- *Eyeshadows in Pewter and Diamant*
- *A lip pencil in Candide*
- *Nail polishes in Jersey and Rouge*
- *Face powder in Translucent Opal*

before they even get into the party season, when they need some evening extras in Velvet and Mallow.

The people who call purple 'aubergine' are very grateful for all of the above.

SUPPORT GROUPS FOR OUR TIMES

- If you were going swimming or to a three-year-old's birthday party, would you take base, concealer, mascara, an eyebrow pencil, a little brush for eyebrow shaping, eyeliner, lipsticks, lip pencils, lip gloss, lip brush, two eyeshadow kits (trios), translucent powder and blusher with you?
- Have you ever snuck out of a man's bedroom at 4a.m. in order to re-apply any of the above?
- Are you pretty convinced that your eyes look a little bit piggy without make-up?

Sounds like you're the kind of gal we're looking for at *Anti-Natural-Look International*. Meet artifice-loving women like yourself. Get the support you deserve from people who understand that you can't even go down for the post without whacking a bit of black round those eye rims. Swap shading tips, lip-line tit-bits and highlighting ideas in very well-lit facilities.

ALL NEW MEMBERS *receive our Will Not Budge, Will Not Smudge, Will-Not-Come-Off-Even-If-You-Attack-It-With-Paint-Stripper Eyelash Dye Kit absolutely free.*

Willing To Exchange
Short blonde crop for set of full length pre-Raphaelite curls.

nineteen

hair care

There are two kinds of women in the world, the ones who have thick, shiny hair with a hint of a wave and a deep, rich, natural colour, and the ones we like.

Most women, of the ordinary mortal variety, are locked in combat with their hair much of the time. In fact, the more money a woman has, the more of it she is prepared to give to someone, anyone, who might be able to fulfil the following elusive fantasy for her ...

The Haircut which on first viewing induces neither tears in the cuttee nor violence towards the cutter. The Haircut which does not induce in the cuttee the overwhelming desire to grab a hairbrush or a hat and rush home. The Haircut which does not make the cuttee's ears look like something over-exposed and a bit rude. The Haircut which doesn't look like a Haircut. In short, The Haircut which makes the cuttee look *unlike* an ordinary mortal woman.

Sometimes a woman has this fantasy fulfilled. But, as she gazes happily at her transformed self, and hands over the entire contents of her wallet in a contented daze, there is always a niggly thought needling away at her new-found bliss. It's this:

'Will I be able to do it myself?'

The woman asks the person who created this mini miracle for her,

'Will I be able to do it myself?'

and the mini-miracle worker says,

'Ooh yes'

and then shows her how. During the course of this showing, the mini-miracle worker does something with his or her fingers at approximately the speed of light. The woman feels her ordinary mortal self creeping up on her. But she is determined not to be deterred. She might lack speed-of-light-digits but she does have access to other aids in the Keeping The Fabulous Fantasy Hairdo Looking Fabulously Fantastic At Home war. Products.

Examples Of Products

- *Some stuff that you put on your hair which puts vitamin B into it (to make it more proactive)*
- *Some stuff which is made out of silk worms (to make it more silky, silly)*
- *Some light and sticky, fluffy stuff, like shaving foam, which you put onto your hand and then onto your hair so that it will be light and fluffy like shaving foam. It will also be a bit sticky. So will your hand*
- *Some stuff made of mountain rainwater that will rid your hair of the sticky stuff*
- *Something that you spray onto your hair which will coat each and every strand with something very scientific and join up all the bits that are broken so as to pump up the volume*
- *Something made of plants which gives hair (clothing, pillow slips, towels and bathroom floors) a deep, rich, natural colour*

Plus . . . waxes, gels, jellies, deep-heat treatments and seaweed-based serums which prevent hair from being damaged by Equipment.

Most hair Equipment looks like something out of an unwatchable scene in a film about prisoners of war. It ends up in the back of a cupboard, covered in a light coating of dust and damaged hair. Each piece represents an afternoon of hope and about £17.99.

get thru' it with: fairies@in between stage

Good Looks All sizes. Immediate Delivery.

twenty

trying some quick-fix beauty tricks

A lot of women spend a lot of money on products, equipment, goo and gadgets which promise to have some sort of beautifying effect in under thirty days. A lot of women do not want to wait that long.

Particular examples of women who do not want to wait that long would be models and beauty queens. That is why there is no shortage of magazine articles called Beauty Secrets Of . . . (models and beauty queens). Women lap these up. Here are some of the models' and beauty queens' secrets:

- *M.'s and B.Q.'s enhance their cleavages with blusher*
- *M.'s and B.Q.'s apply hemorrhoid treatments to pesky eye puffiness and toothpaste to troublesome zits*
- *B.Q.'s prevent their swimsuits from riding by applying hairspray, strategically*
- *M.'s swear by Eight-hour Cream and a black cashmere wrap for pretty much any beauty emergency*

Unfortunately, women are usually unable to unearth enough hints and tips from these articles to turn themselves into someone resembling a model or a beauty queen by Friday night, so they have to look further afield Quick-fix-beauty-tricks-wise.

Every now and then a man or a fly-on-the-wall documentary film maker or someone with an excellent scientific brain has a bash at explaining to women that Quick-fix Beauty Tricks are a waste of time at £45.

These explanations do not make a dent in a woman's enthusiasm. In fact, a woman who has just spent a dismal afternoon trying on ill-fitting swimsuits has absolutely no truck with them whatsoever. She's willing to try anything. Also, and this is something often overlooked by men, women enjoy these things. They think they're fun.

Examples Of Quick-fix Beauty Tricks Which Women Think Are Fun

- *Booking yourself a course of lying on a machine which sends tiny electric shocks into the thigh and buttock region*
- *Paying someone to cover you with algae*
- *Paying someone to wrap you in cold bandages*
- *Having high-pressure hoses aimed at your flabby bits*
- *Being encased in mud*
- *Being rubbed all over with something gritty*

As a general rule, the more money women have, the more of these things they do. In fact, lots of women's idea of a long weekend holiday treat is to go to a place where they can have all these things done at once and they are only allowed to eat brown rice. This kind of experience costs about a week's salary.

Sometimes, a modern woman who is on the super-fast track to pin-skinny skips brown rice and goes straight for Flushing Out Her Toxins. This involves a lot of mineral water and a few grapes. There are serious Toxin Flushers who go to places where a hose is aimed very specifically in the buttock region by someone in a white coat. Even outside California there are female folks who've convinced themselves that *this* is fun.

Nobody thinks that plastic surgery is fun but, in terms of something permanently beautifying in under thirty days, it has its appealing side, so lots of women consider it. Women tend to consider plastic surgery more often in the summer. In California it is summer almost all the time so that tells you something. A lot more

women would consider plastic surgery, even in Finland, if it cost less than £45 and it didn't hurt. Another thing which is a bit off-putting is the number of documentaries on BBC2 about deformed females who are suing their surgeons for GBH. This means that a lot of women just make do with reading something called *Diary Of A Face Lift* on their summer hols. After a woman has read something like this she is not beyond having a bit of practice at pulling her face backwards by tugging sharply at the hair at her temples, sucking her cheeks in and checking out her reflection in the bathroom mirror. Mostly she is fairly bored when she does this. If she is bored and almost forty she does it a bit more seriously. If she is bored and almost forty and she has been on summer hols with someone who is almost twenty-three, she sometimes does it with a seriousness bordering on the obsessive.

Handbag Clearance
Everything must go.

twenty-one

having a clearout

Quite often when a woman goes out to buy herself some super-duper extra-lengthening, no-gooey-residue, glamour-lash mascara, she discovers that it comes with a diddy liddle bag of teeny tiny goodies (which she will never use), absolutely gratis as long as she spends another £14.99 on a glossy-pot-for-lips (which she needs anyway).

Women cannot resist diddy liddle bags of teeny tiny gratis goodies. Mostly the diddy liddle bags end up in the back of a cupboard covered with dust and unused hair equipment.

Other Things Which Women Keep In The Cupboard With The Unused Hair Equipment

- *A diddy liddle bag of teeny tiny gratis goodies from an airline*
- *A massage mitt which diminishes cellulite if used for fifteen minutes on a daily basis for thirty consecutive days*
- *Something for removing nail cuticles*
- *Nail polish which has gone sticky*

- *Something made of something natural for removing unwanted hair naturally*
- *Some sachets of gratis goodies torn out of magazines (with bits of magazine page stuck to them)*

Women can never understand why men insist on keeping their school cricket sweaters and a holey old hat.

The woman keeps her new extra-lengthening mascara in a quilted, plastic-lined bag. This bag is not very diddy. It won't fit in the cupboard so she puts it on the floor next to her dressing table. It is full of part-used things with once adorable packaging and gooey residues of various hues.

Every now and then a woman reads in a Women's Beauty Bible that you can only keep things with gooey residues for forty-seven days without risking something hideous that happened to a lab rabbit. Sometimes this inspires her to have a bit of a clearout.

Still, even during a good old clearout (which takes a while on account of the necessity for double-checking that that Tasty Tangerine gloss pot really does make your teeth, skin and whites of eyes look puke yellow despite its adorable packaging), a woman can never quite bring herself to chuck out the liddle diddy dusty bitties. She figures they'll come in very handy should she suddenly find herself jetting off to a five-star resort in Mauritius.

Sometimes a clearout extends to a handbag. In cases like these a woman is suddenly inspired to heft her handbag onto her lap, root about in its cavernous interior for a few minutes and then remove two possibly used, possibly just disintegrated-via-a-natural-decaying-process tissues, along with some form of menstrual protection that has taken on a very odd shape and a peppermint that looks like it would do for any poor lab rabbit unfortunate enough to come in contact with it, and chuck them.

The next day the woman gets an attack of the sneezes, her period starts early and she has to kiss someone after she's eaten salad with onions in it, so she's not tempted to do anything this rash again for quite some time.

FAIRY GODMOTHERS FOR OUR TIMES
So, despite the fact that this adorable handbag only measures 3x4 inches, it still contains everything you could possibly need
cabfare
tissues
make-up
more make-up
Spare knickers
little Grace-Kelly cardy
Peppermints
Snap-shots of ex
Curling Tongs
tights
BENDY tampons
www: mary poppins.co.party town

Found Five extra kilos. Rightful owner please call to arrange collection.

twenty-two

dieting

Modern women will tell you that they are all over that thinness business. Codswallop. Most women would like to be a wee bit lighter. They'd like their tummies to be tighter and their bottoms *not* to stick out. Lots of them want to be slim. They suspect that therein lies Happiness.

If a woman spends a lousy afternoon trying on trousers without finding a pair that flatter her rear, a steely determination tends to come over her and she goes on a diet.

In the olden days women attempted to burn off calories with grapefruit. Nowadays calorie counting is out. The fashionable lass goes on a diet where you eat red peppers and chicken on a Tuesday and you mustn't eat anything green on a Wednesday. (Also, you *must* eat the fruit before the egg on the Friday.) A woman who is absolutely determined to slim down because

a) she has met a new man
b) she is going on holiday
c) she has just come back from holiday and picked up her snapshots
d) it is January 1st

can keep this sort of thing going for about five days. Then she starts to get fed up with trying to remember whether it's No rice with fish or No lima beans with lentils. It's a bore constantly having to refer to the four photocopied pages of notes.

She starts to cheat.

Examples Of Cheating

- *Making a nice, creamy, white sauce to add to your Weight Watchers' grilled chicken*
- *Eating your nutritious meal replacements as between-meal snacks*
- *Not counting slices of bread and cappuccinos*
- *Not counting the second Weight Watchers' grilled chicken*
- *Leaving the cabbage out of the cabbage soup diet*

Once the woman has started to cheat it isn't usually very long before she decides that the whole business is probably a bit of a waste of time.

Things (that she now considers were probably a bit of a waste of time) That An Otherwise Sensible Woman Has Done In An Attempt To Drop A Couple Of Kilos

- *Run around in her flat wearing clingfilm*
- *Invested in an outfit two sizes too small – as an incentive*
- *Invested in a juicer*
- *Dined for seven consecutive evenings on something packaged in cardboard which tasted of cardboard*
- *Bought a book with the words Fibre or Bikini in the title*
- *Drunk three gins ... with slimline tonic*
- *Bought and actually swallowed something called Fat Ban*
- *Bought and used something which does exactly what Fat Ban does While-U-Sleep*
- *Thought Thin*
- *Put a picture of herself looking svelte, two summers ago, on the fridge*
- *Put a picture of Claudia Schiffer, looking like she always looks, on the fridge*
- *Put a sticky label with the word No written on it on the fridge*
- *Bought some super-high-tech-any-itty-bit-of-a-pound-detecting scales and put them in the bathroom*

Luckily a woman usually discovers, eventually, that she can get more or less the effect she wants by only ever weighing herself first thing in the morning (stark naked, with empty bowel and bladder and one hand pressing gently on the towel rail) and investing in a black trouser suit with quite a long jacket. After this she only has short lapses during which she walks the long way to the station in order to avoid places that sell Mars Bars.

'FAIRY GODMOTHERS FOR OUR TIMES'
But it will only be activated if you cram something made of 2/3 lard and 1/3 chocolate into your mouth, whole when you're not even hungry
get help@will power.co.slim city

Second hand Well-upholstered thighs (pair). In need of some improvement.

twenty-three

exercising

All women have tried to exercise. This is because in their hearts they know that exercise:

a) is good for you
b) makes you look better in a swimsuit
(The second of these tends to be the more inspirational when it comes to stomach crunchers.)

Anyway, the world is forever coming up with new ways to make the trying exercise process more appealing. Fitness fads sweep urban centres in the same way that skipping and knitting swept the classrooms of our girlhood. A woman gives samba a bash, and then yoga. She considers sending away for something made of plastic and elastic (which will result in a terrifically toned body in just thirty days, £22.99 plus p&p). She decides against it. She decides against the slidy thigh-worker thingy that you can set up in the privacy of your own home, too. She tears out an ad for exercycles, which she keeps. But then, eventually, she decides to join a gym.

As soon as a woman joins a gym she buys some exercising outfits. (The fashionable lass gets herself nice, cottony, casual-type stuff that looks like she's had it for ages. Around £22.45 apiece.) Then she signs up for Aqua Aerobics, Morning Jump Start, Evening Stretch and a personal fitness assessment with her own personal fitness assessor who shows her how to use the slidy thigh-worker thingies and pieces of plasticy elastic in the gym. About a squillion other people are sweating it out in this gym at the time.

The woman begins a routine of schlepping determinedly from the office to the locker room on a regular basis. She usually announces that she is doing this to quite a lot of people. She says how good she feels. This is true. For a while.

The thing is, there is something a bit off-putting about other people sweating. Also, now that the Morning Jump Start group is changing to Tuesday it's *impossible* to get to it. Plus, have you seen the size of the thighs on that woman who teaches Bums 'n' Tums? It's all a bit of a downer. The lass, no matter how fashionable, usually begins to give the gym a miss.

Some women keep going to the gym. They start to take going-to-the-gym *really* seriously. They are oblivious to the other sweating souls. They wear Lycra. The haul themselves onto the Super-High-Tech-Thigh-Inflaming-Runner-Thingy and they crank it right up. They start to run. They keep on running. From the expression on their faces you'd think they were running for their lives.

Yes, well, blow that for a game of soldiers.

Most women find the slope to total exercise abstinence is a short and easily slipped one.

Some Things That Women Buy (in addition to nice cottony gym gear and a million-pound-a-minute gym membership) Before They Slip The Slope To Total Exercise Abstinence

- *A swimsuit you can swim in (as opposed to one that looks nice)*
- *Shoes that you can run in which don't look particularly nice either*
- *Shoes that you can tap/flamenco/samba dance in which look quite nice actually*
- *A super water-sports-proof Walkman*
- *A rucksack*
- *A leotard*

- *Cycling shorts*
- *A skipping rope*
- *A tennis/badminton/squash racket*
- *A minimum-bounce bra*
- *A video in which everybody bounces a lot*

There is usually a cupboard in a woman's house which is a shrine to her good intentions.

SUPPORT GROUPS FOR OUR TIMES

- Do you suspect that if you started exercising again you might overcome the increase in body weight, slightly distended belly, tiredness, inability to sleep, stress-related irritability, slackening of muscle tone, shortness of breath, general loss of strength and thickening of thigh area that you are currently experiencing?
- Are you plagued with twinges of self-loathing whenever you spend a Sunday afternoon crashed out on the sofa wearing the jogging pants and sweatshirt you bought to wear to aerobics?
- Do you feel a little bit sick whenever you see that expensive health-club membership card lying unused at the bottom of your handbag?

Take out a subscription to *Ex Lapse*. No meetings. No sweat. Just a regular newsletter for people tormented by Gym Guilt. We guarantee that after just one leisurely peruse you'll be hooked and, what's more, absolutely convinced that Exercise Is Really Bad For You. Read others' harrowing experiences, such as 'Aqua club turned my hair green' and 'My shower verucca horror'. Convince others of insidious exercise dangers like the Lycra-leotard-yeast-infection link.

SEND FOR *our reassuring Common Cartilage Injuries issue today.*

Now In Stock Dead fish. Make terrific miracle cures.

twenty-four

swallowing supplements

Supplements are things you need to take to make up for the fact that your diet consists primarily of chocolate oranges and low-cal cardboard dinners. Also you have been using up a lot of energy schlepping from the office to the gym on public transport three times a week, carrying half a ton of gym gear. Old-fashioned women, or perfectly ordinary women on an ordinary Tuesday, are likely to consider that the occasional chewy vitamin C is pretty much adequate Supplement-wise, but every now and then most modern women become quite convinced re the benefits of fish oil.

Examples Of Supplements That A Woman Has Sworn By

- *Something made of seaweed*
- *Something made of tree bark*
- *Something made of cactus*
- *Something made of toadstools*
- *Something made of the root of a common roadside plant*
- *Something which combines every vitamin known to man with the essence of pressed flower stamens*
- *Something made of garlic*

A woman is rarely wedded to one particular Supplement, no matter how heartily she swears by it at first. This pattern of behaviour is encouraged by magazine articles called Ten Ways To Optimum Health. Sometimes a woman reads one of these articles with a friend. In circumstances like these one friend has to hold still while the other one figures out which bit of her foot corresponds to her kidneys or whether her irises are indicating a digestive system overloaded with copper. At the end of the article there is always a long list of ever more obscure supplements, spelt with the letters Q and X. A woman doesn't mind. She likes to run the gamut. This is what she does.

She buys a thirty-day supply of something and then she swallows this thing religiously for twelve days. On the thirteenth day she forgets, but that's OK because she remembers again on about the eighteenth day. Then she takes the Supplement again for about five

more days or until she has a nasty gagging experience or a mid-morning nausea attack or she hears some dire story about somebody else's kidney stones (whichever is the sooner) and then she stops taking it. There are still quite a few days' worth of supply left in the jar. They stay there for a very long time. They are still there seven weeks later when the woman puts the new jar of the latest thing she swears by in the cupboard next to them.

Women tend to apply the buy-and-keep-what's-left-of-the-old-supply policy to quite a few things. This is particularly true of things that you keep in bathrooms. This is even more particularly true of things that come in nice packaging that you keep in bathrooms. A charitable woman might admit that this is one of the reasons why men who live with women can never find the aspirin by themselves.

'FAIRY GODMOTHERS FOR OUR TIMES'
Your daughter is an adult... Your daughter is an adult... she can't see me, she's only aware of the gentle lilt of my voice... Your daughter is...
www: martyrs.co.gritted teeth

Reward for return of twenty-fifth birthday.

twenty-five

staying young

There are an awful lot of modern women who are well over the age of twenty-two whose lives have changed precious little since they were. Today's young woman gets to cling to youth for what seems like an age to her mother. Some mothers point this kind of thing out to women on a pretty monotonous basis. A mother worries. This is what she says to her daughter. 'Your father worries.' Here are some of the things that a daughter is doing (well after her twenty-second birthday) that her mother says her father worries about:

- *Living in a tiny flat with a walk-up and badly kept common parts*
- *Going on holidays, for weeks at a time, with her girlfriends*
- *Spending whatever money she's got left from buying clothes on CDs and not saving a penny*
- *Leaving her job on a whim*
- *Coming home for the weekend looking ridiculous, wearing an outfit that no one would ever give her a decent job in with her hair dyed blonde*
- *Showing absolutely no sign of getting married*

Here are just some of the things that a daughter is doing that would cause her parents to have an apoplectic fit if they had the slightest inkling:

- *relying on her horoscope for advice about her future*
- *drinking, alone, with friends and with men that no one would think of as marriage material*
- *considering moving to Sydney*

The thing is that, as a rule, women do not want to be told that life will be wonderful and they'll win an Oscar when they are sixty, and very few women under the age of forty think that meeting a man who has absolutely nothing wrong with him when they are fifty will be all that much fun. Actually, no matter how many middle-aged style icons the beauty bibles come up with, lots of women think that a wonderful life is a wee bit wasted on anyone who can't wear whatever Cameron Diaz is wearing.

So, while women can't cheat the actual years, which march relentlessly on no matter how much money is spent on AHA-based formulations, they figure they might be able to fight forty as long as they don't give in to the kind of lifestyle their mothers think would be good for them. Hence the number of women in wine bars on Friday nights, and cinemas on Sundays, and sunny islands in June, dressed as Cameron Diaz.

One night, though, when a woman is a good way on from twenty-two, she is lying in her old single bed in her old room in her mother's and father's house. Her trendy towny outfit is lying over the back of a chair, looking forlorn. She is secretly, worriedly, wondering whether her new blonde locks and wispy, waspy haircut are really quite as flattering as she thought. Is it, perhaps, time to take note of what her upper arms and increasingly lower bottom are telling her? Is it only a

matter of time before someone, other than her father, tells her that funky isn't funny any more? Should she settle down, move out of the centre of town, buy a house, a sensible trouser suit and a dinner-party dress, and then invest seriously in a pension?

As a general rule a woman hot-foots it back to her flat the morning after a thought like this, calls a friend and concocts a plan to spend several weeks in January in a land where the sun shines all the time. Somewhere, deep in their collective subconscious, these women believe that this plan will increase the odds that they'll win an Oscar and meet a man who has absolutely nothing wrong with him in the very near future. Nobody smart mentions any of this to her mother.

Temporary Let
Hum-drum existence.
Owner going abroad.

twenty-six

going on holiday

Going On Holiday involves some of women's favourite things. For example:

- *Sunshine*

When young modern women go on holiday they don't usually go on a fascinating European tour of twenty-one museums and cathedrals. Mostly they go somewhere sunny. Very few men understand the uplifting effect that a plan to go somewhere sunny has on most women. Before women get to the sunny place they are so busy with hair removal and body-lotion, fake-tan and waterproof-mascara purchasing that blue Monday mornings are completely banished.

Women vow that when they get to the sunny place they will eat fish, always wear a hat and do some exercise every day. There are probably some women who stick to this plan. There are lots more who drink sangria at lunch on the second day and don't do much besides sunbathing and easy reading thereafter.

The thing is, sunbathing and easy reading are great, but a woman likes a little something to liven up the evenings. Luckily, holidays offer lots of opportunity for:

♦ *Getting dressed up and going out*

Women love this. The truth is that, lots of times, a woman enjoys the Getting Dressed Up part as much as the Going Out part and, on holiday, Getting Dressed Up is extra specially fun because she has been planning her outfits for three months (or since she booked the holiday, whichever is the longer). Quite a lot of these outfits are new. The woman bought them in-between waterproof-mascara forays. There are approximately thirty-seven of them. Unless the woman is on holiday with a man, in which case there are forty-two, plus shoes. If a woman is on holiday with another woman the thirty-seven automatically becomes seventy-four, on account of borrowing, which adds to the fun no end. These outfits were generally chosen with a body-lotioned, fake-tanned, only fish-fed and exercised body in mind. Sometimes they're a bit tight. Sometimes they're a bit bright. Sometimes they're not the sort of thing a woman would wear at home. A woman who's been sunbathing for a week is not usually worrying very much about this when she hits the bar without a bra on. This is one of the effects of:

♦ *Changing location*

Women are Changing Location fans. There are blue Monday mornings when a woman thinks that moving to New York, New Delhi or New Zealand would be the answer to all her ills. However, by Monday evening this plan usually seems a bit drastic, whereas two glorious weeks on a beach somewhere is wonderfully within reach. A lot of modern women have the wherewithal to get themselves from Manchester to Morocco.

The thing is that since two glorious beach weeks require about as much preparation as permanent emigration to Idaho a woman sometimes forgets that life will go on afterwards. On the few occasions when she does give being-back-in-the-same-old-location-again any thought, she imagines herself with her tanned, lotioned, only fish-fed and exercised body. In short, looking much more like Cameron Diaz. Which means that Monday mornings will probably be magically transformed anyway.

If the holiday concerned is a woman's honeymoon this kind of thinking can be the starting point for some Monday-morning blues that stretch well into the following weekend.

SUPPORT GROUPS FOR OUR TIMES

- Have you ever shoved some shoes that go with only one thing you own, a zip-up thing full of accessories and a very heavy towelling robe (which could be useful to put around you when you're coming back from the pool) into the suitcase which already wouldn't close without the application of severe brute force?
- Are you all-too-familiar with the following phrases:

  'You brought it so you can carry it.'
  'We're going for two weeks not two years.'
  'What have you got in here, a * body?'***

- Have you ever wondered whether it might be a good idea to take your own pillows?

Give *Overpackers Anonymous* a call. OA is a caring group of excess-weight watchers who once, just like you, risked divorce or dislocated shoulders every time we went on holiday.

In future, avoid decapitating fellow travellers with your hand luggage by phoning our 24-hour helpline before you overfill that sports bag with bulky, non-essential items. And ditch with confidence the oversized straw hat (that you have to carry everywhere in case it gets squashed) by following our unique Just Say You Don't Need It programme.

CONTACT US TODAY *and see a new travel-lite quicker than you can say: Capsule Wardrobe*

Movie Stars wanted.No previous experience necessary. Hours to suit.

twenty-seven

doing a bit of freelance

More women than will ever admit it have a bit of a schizoid approach to working. It's not that a woman isn't into her career, mostly she's just as keen as any man when it comes to getting on job-wise. It's just that she has a few more opt-out options. On a grey, nothing-to-wear morning, it is not unusual for her to give these options a bit of thought.

Most female opt-out options have to do with babies, but childless women who find that nine to five is getting them down can usually think of other ways of staying housebound. For example, being kept like an old-fashioned mistress. In the wet-midweek-morning fantasy this plan does not involve an unattractive man with sweaty hands and a dingy downtown hideaway. Still, even if the man in this plan is Mr Pitt, and the hideaway is Hawaii, today's woman tends to give up on the Mistress idea pretty quick. It smacks of a lack of independence.

Being kept like a thoroughly modern wife has a bit more appeal. When a woman is being lashed by rain in a trainless station this option can seem quite realistic, even if she hasn't met a single man without dandruff in eighteen months.

But despite the delights that being able to pop off to yoga and the shops whenever you wanted might bring, most modern women like having their own money. That's why they eventually alight upon the idea of working part-time.

The working part-time fantasy perfectly combines the personal paycheque with the possibility of lovely long lunches with chums, fun with the kids and time to pursue other interests.

Re Other Interests: Most women have Other Interests, i.e. interests outside of their work. Sometimes these interests are of the domestic variety like cooking and kids, sometimes they are of the sports variety like tennis and skiing, sometimes they are of the artistic variety like watercolours and poetry and sometimes they are the adventure and travel kind. So far these interests are pretty similar to those of men.

But a woman tends to need a bit more than just the weekend or the odd weekday evening to pursue her Other Interests. For one thing she is generally a bit more busy popping in to M&S and buying birthday cards on a Saturday morning than a man is. Also, no man has ever needed to spend precious out-of-office minutes arranging to have some shoes dyed, getting a bikini wax, or finding a moisturiser that isn't greasy. Plus, he does not usually spend a great deal of time lost in thoughts like these: 'If I ring him will he think I'm pushy?' and 'Should I get a fringe cut?'

When the smart modern woman says she'd like to work part-time she doesn't mean she'd like to be a part-time meat-packer. Ideally she'd like something part-time in the glamour industries. An extra bonus with regard to part-time jobs in the glamour industries is that you don't even have to say you work part-time. You can say you're doing a bit of freelance.

Examples Of Glamour Industries In Which A Lot Of Women Would Like To Be Doing A Bit Of Freelance

- *Books*
- *Mags*
- *Movies*
- *Pop*
- *Frocks*
- *Objects d'Art*
- *Telly*
- *Modelling*
- *Organising Sports Events*

It doesn't matter how many times some woman says, on a chat show, that doing a bit of freelance in these industries is *not actually* terribly glamorous *at all*, it always looks pretty damn appealing to a part-time meat-packer.

Credit Cards
Already chopped up.
Free delivery.

twenty-eight budgeting

Female Financial Planning has its own logic. Men do not always understand this logic, which is why a woman who lives with a man sometimes doesn't bother him with details like, for example, why she bought a pair of leopardskin boots twelve hours after she told him that she couldn't afford her car tax.

Here is a conversation which most women are very familiar with and most men couldn't fathom:

'Fabulous, huh?'

'Fabulous.'

'Sixty per cent off. Unbelievable.'

'Unbelievable. Will you wear it on Saturday?'

'No. It doesn't fit.'

A man *cannot* understand that we will invest in shoes that induce gangrene simply for the thrill of owning them.

Women have so many more daily temptations where budget breaking is concerned. Lipsticks, lotions, lavender oil, boots that match bags, tights that match boots . . . which is why easy credit is so appealing. Shops-that-sell-frocks (and all the other flotsam that is the female lot in life) have not been slow to catch on to this fact. They offer a woman plastic quicker than you can say matching belt.

Most modern women hear the sound of plastic-related bills falling, fat, onto their doormats on a regular basis. Lots of modern women open the envelopes and add up the available credit. They like to think of the window between balance and limit as Spending Money.

It's a rare woman who adds up the lines titled 'interest'. Most of us would prefer not to know how much a must-have Christmas outfit has cost on minimum payments by the following December.

Some women have a 'special stash'. Usually they don't include this money in 'available cash'. Women do not want to pay off debts with their rainy-day dosh. This is true even if the amounts due on their cards are charging up interest at triple the rate their savings are making.

A woman, as a rule, likes to see something for her money. Something nice. A musty statement with a nil balance or a pension payment paid just doesn't cut the mustard where fun with finance is concerned. After all, 'Money Management' – what a dull little phrase it is when compared with, say, 'Meet me at Harvey Nichols.'

This desire to have something lovely to hold means that many a woman with a new abode invests in an apple-green sofa (and cushions that match) a wee while before she deals with the dry rot. It wouldn't be absolutely off-base to claim, either, that her eyes glazed over when the mortgage rep mentioned tax relief. She was busy wondering where she could get a big pine chest for the guest bedroom.

Of course, a woman says that the masculine style with money has its down-side too. She's right. By and large it's men who lose homes at poker and men who get themselves into million-quid hock.

Meanwhile, we go on thinking that we're awfully wise if we manage to disguise mince as something grander, or an Oxfam buy as designer chic. We keep looking blank when asked about our banking arrangements, telling little lies about prices (£39.99) and spending mini mints on eye creams and colour schemes, while moaning about gas bills (due) and giving you (blokes) a really hard time for forking out for super-wide-screen-picture-within-picture-state-of-the-art eyesores when a simple little portable would do.

'FAIRY GODMOTHERS FOR OUR TIMES'
It's a Speaks Your Balance credit card
£200... Plus Interest makes £250 ... Oh boy, 300 Big Ones
thrift fairies@save something.co.economy drive

Easy going outlook sought. View listening to music and long walks on the beach.

twenty-nine

stress relief

Here is a woman's little trouser-buying dilemma – if she opts for something woolly, and therefore warm, the woolly inside will scratch. If she opts for something woolly, warm and lined, the lining will make her thighs feel fat. This is an example of the sort of little worry that never besets a man.

More Examples Of Little Worries That Never Beset Men

- *Laddered tights*
- *Cellulite*
- *Scaly shins*
- *Speculums*
- *Bikini waxes*
- *Cramps*
- *Slippy bra-straps*
- *Smudged mascara*
- *Fine eye-lines*
- *Bust size*

- *Loving too much*
- *Walking in heels*
- *What to wear*
- *Where to leave your handbag*

If you added work and remembering birthdays to this list, if you added quite a bit of cooking and looking after the house, if you added Christmas or kids and trying to find a carpark at the supermarket on Saturdays, you would begin to see how a modern woman might be suffering from a bit of Stress.

When women are suffering from Stress the ten-day break they had in Greece in June seems woefully inadequate in terms of tension release. This is especially true if they spent this break bickering with some bloke about windsurfing.

A Stressed-out woman feels the need to find herself a more effective means of relaxation. *Forty* days in Greece might fit the bill but bosses and bank managers (not to mention blokes) generally conspire against a woman with regard to this plan. She has to resort to putting something made out of squished-up pine needles in the bath water instead.

A locked bathroom door and a load of squished-up pine needles don't always do the trick, but that's OK because lots of people all over the world have spotted the niche in the Stressed-out Women market. So the Stressed-out woman can light a lavender candle to ease her mind at night, or she can choose to have someone's thumbs stuck in her pressure points or be shut in a tank full of salty water. She can go to some classes which involve a bit of mild contortionism and a lot of lying on your sleeping bag listening to the sounds of the rain forest, or some sessions of lying on a narrow bed being rubbed down with yinny yangy oils and listening to the sounds of sea mammals giving birth.

The modern woman laps this stuff up. Still, if it fails, she tends to have a less New Age approach in her arsenal. In her handbag, actually. It's this: sugar-coated-super-power-pain-relief drug candy.

Neuroticofen. Whips stress-head in a minute. Costs about as much as forty days in Greece.

SUPPORT GROUPS FOR OUR TIMES

- Are you experiencing frenzies, tizzies, paddies, tantrums, panic attacks, crankiness, tears, scowls, growls, giggles, snarls, howling and loud bursts of hollow laughter in, say, your lunch hour?
- Have you noticed your loved ones, workmates and people who might have considered stealing your parking space slowly backing away from you and looking nervous?
- Do you ever suspect that you might be mad, deranged or just plain crazy before coming to the conclusion that you're actually absolutely miserable and that if you could just get some sleep, service, sex, red wine, sweet food and sensible answers everything would be wonderful and you could overcome the constant urge to scream?

Yes? No? Oh, all right? Then *Mood Swingers* is the answer to your pointless ranting.

Join others in a padded environment for a few happy hours of riding the emotional roller-coaster. Come along to one of our hysterical get-togethers. We meet every twenty-eight days to weep with rage and finish off the evening with a fun bout of euphoria.

(Please leave sharp objects at the door.)

Wanted P/time soulmate. Mostly evenings.

thirty

depending on friends

Women have all sorts of friends. For example:

- ***Work friends***
  Know more about your personal life than almost anyone in the world on account of overhearing all your phone calls. Never come to your house
- ***Old friends***
  Know your mother. Remember what you looked like at school. Have two children (one is your Godchild), a husband (a bit dull) and a house which is twenty-seven train stops from where you live. Which is why you've slightly lost touch, personal-life-wise (and Godchild's-birthday-wise)
- ***New best friends***
  Know absolutely everything about you, isn't that amazing, just as if you'd known each other for ages. Have a powerful influence on hair, hobbies and frock sense (for about three months)

but the real super-bond female friendships occur between women who are able to have a really good time together without ever feeling the need to hold their stomachs in. Women know that women all over the world have these kinds of friendships because women's magazines periodically run stories about them.

Other Stories That Women's Magazines Run Periodically

- *How to put blusher on the apple of your cheek*
- *Where to wear the stripes on your swimsuit if you are pear-shaped*
- *How to transform a chest of drawers for under £22.99*
- *How to slough off dull winter skin with a loofah*
- *How to make a Valentine's breakfast*
- *What kind of sunglasses the stars are wearing*

In the magazine story 'Why I Love My Friends', two very famous or glamorous caring-and-sharing female creatures say, 'You can really be yourself with your women friends.' Which every woman knows means you never have to hold your stomach in, among other things.

A woman's friends are there whenever her boss is being a meany. A woman's friends stand by her when she blows her last bucks on shoes. A woman's friends don't mind if she goes on a diet of grapes and Evian water or fails her driving test or cries whenever life hands her lemons. None of them would date a bloke who did the same.

But a bit of a double standard is OK because women know that friendships with other women have advantages that relationships with men don't have. (Apart from the stomach-holding-in business.) Women feel that they can depend on their friends at times when men are less than reliable.

Times When Men Are Less Than Reliable

- *When someone is crying*
- *When something has happened that a woman needs to know about*
- *When a woman wants a plain black cashmere sweater, size 12 with a V-neck, for Christmas*
- *When a woman is waiting by the phone*

Some women have a Heterosexual Male Friend who is completely dependable and doesn't seem to mind about stomachs, held in or otherwise. Quite often this man becomes a sort of honorary woman friend. The woman feels she can share her personal life with him. Before long she tells him that there are no decent men out there.

Now that she's met a man
it's 'we this' 'we that'
... she's completely lost her sense of independence

LADIES